RUNAWAY

Also by JORIE GRAHAM

RUNAWAY

New Poems

JORIE GRAHAM

An Imprint of HarperCollins*Publishers*

RUNAWAY. Copyright © 2020 by Jorie Graham. All rights reserved. Printed in the United States of America. No part of this book may be used or reproduced in any manner whatsoever without written permission except in the case of brief quotations embodied in critical articles and reviews. For information, address HarperCollins Publishers, 195 Broadway, New York, NY 10007.

HarperCollins books may be purchased for educational, business, or sales promotional use. For information, please email the Special Markets Department at SPsales@harpercollins.com.

Ecco® and HarperCollins® are trademarks of HarperCollins Publishers.

A hardcover edition of this book was published in 2020 by Ecco, an imprint of Harper-Collins Publishers.

FIRST ECCO PAPERBACK EDITION PUBLISHED 2021

Designed by Erica Mena

Library of Congress Cataloging-in-Publication Data has been applied for.

ISBN 978-0-06-303671-0 (pbk.)

21 22 23 24 25   LSC   10 9 8 7 6 5 4 3 2 1

For Samantha Lorraine Almanza

ACKNOWLEDGMENTS

Great thanks to the editors in whose pages these poems first appeared: *The London Review of Books, The New Yorker Magazine, Poetry Magazine, Lana Turner, The New York Review of Books, The Los Angeles Review of Books, Harper's Magazine, Ambit, The Kenyon Review.*

Gratitude to my editor, Daniel Halpern; my designer, Erica Mena; and my copyeditor, Sol Kim Bentley.

Gratefulness every day for the presence in my life of Paul Gordon, Lynn Bell, Ty Romijn, Nancy Berger, Caitlin Cook, Sandra Washburne, Tara Ledden, Lauren Bimmler, Case Kerns, Thomas Neilan, Beverly Moy, Barbara Smith, Jose Baselga, Kenneth Gold, Patrick O'Gara, Chris Gilligan, and Jeffrey Zack.

And to Peter, without whose daily example and love I could not have made this book.

The Gods themselves cannot recall their gifts.

—Tennyson

CONTENTS

I

ALL

Or if then thou gavest me all,
All was but all.

—Donne

After the rain stops you can hear the rained-on.
You hear oscillation, outflowing, slips.
The tipping-down of the branches, the down, the
exact weight of those drops that fell

over the days and nights, their strength, accumulation,
shafting down through the resistant skins,
nothing perfect but then also the exact remain
of sun, the sum

of the last not-yet-absorbed, not-yet-evaporated
days. After the rain stops you hear the
washed world, the as-if-inquisitive garden, the as-if-perfect beginning again
of the buds forced open, forced open—you

cannot not unfurl
endlessly, entirely, till it is the yes of blossom, that end
not end—what does that sound sound like
deep in its own time where it roots us out

completed, till it is done. But it is not done.
Here is still strengthening. Even if only where light
shifts to accord the strange complexity which is beauty.
Each tip in the light end-outreaching as if anxious

but not. The rain stopped. The perfect is not beauty.
Is not a finished thing. Is a making
of itself into more of itself, oozing and pressed
full force out of the not-having-been

into this momentary being—cold, more
sharp, till the beam passes as the rain passed,
tipping into the sound of ending which does not end,
and giving us that sound. We hear it.

We hear it, hands
useless, eyes heavy with knowing we do not
understand it, we hear it, deep in its own
consuming, compelling, a dry delight, a just-going-on sound not

desire, neither lifeless nor deathless, the elixir of
change, without form, we hear you in our world, you not of
our world, though we can peer at (though not into)
flies, gnats, robin, twitter of what dark consolation—

though it could be light, this insistence this morning
unmonitored by praise, amazement, nothing to touch
where the blinding white thins as the flash moves off
what had been just the wide-flung yellow poppy,

the fine day-opened eye of hair at its core,
complex, wrinkling and just, as then the blazing ends, sloughed off as if a
god-garment the head and body
of the ancient flower had put on for a while—

we have to consider the *while* it seems
to say or I seem to say or
something else seems to we are not
nothing.

TREE

Today on two legs stood and reached to the right spot as I saw it
choosing among the twisting branches and multifaceted changing shades,
and greens, and shades of greens, lobed, and lashing sun, the fig that seemed to me the
perfect one, the ready one, it is permitted, it is possible, it is

actual. The VR glasses are not needed yet, not for now, no, not for this while
longer. And it is warm in my cupped palm. And my fingers close round but not too
fast. Somewhere wind like a hammerstroke slows down and lengthens
endlessly. Closer-in the bird whose coin-toss on a metal tray never stills to one

face. Something is preparing to begin again. It is not us. *Shhh* say the spreading sails of
cicadas as the winch of noon takes hold and we are wrapped in day and hoisted
up, all the ribs of time showing through in the growing in the lengthening
harness of sound—some gnats nearby, a fly where the white milk-drop of the

torn stem starts. Dust on the eglantine skin, white powder in the confetti of light
all up the branches, truth, sweetness of blood-scent and hauled-in light, withers of
the wild carnival of tree shaking once as the fruit is torn from its dream. Remain I
think backing away from the trembling into full corrosive sun. Momentary blindness

follows. Correction. There are only moments. They hurt. Correction. Must I put down
here that this is long ago. That the sky has been invisible for years now. That the ash
of our fires has covered the sun. That the fruit is stunted yellow mold when it appears
at all and we have no produce to speak of. No longer exists. All my attention is

free for you to use. I can cast farther and farther out, before the change, a page turned,
we have gone into another story, history floundered or one day the birds dis-
appeared. The imagination tried to go here when we asked it to, from where I hold the
fruit in my right hand, but it would not go. Where is it now. Where is this *here* where

you and I look up trying to make sense of the normal, turn it to life, more life, disinterred from desire, heaved up onto the dry shore awaiting the others who could not join us in the end. For good. I want to walk to the left around this tree I have made again. I want to sit under it full of secrecy insight immensity vigor bursting complexity

swarm. Oh great forwards and backwards. I never felt my face change into my new face. Where am I facing now. Is the question of good still stinging the open before us with its muggy destination pitched into nothingness? Something expands in you where it wrenches-up its bright policing into view—is this good, is this the good—

under the celebrating crowd, inside the silences it forces hard away all round itself, where chanting thins, where we win the war again, made thin by bravery and belief, here's a polaroid if you want, here's a souvenir, here now for you to watch unfold, up close, the fruit is opening, the ribs will widen now, it is all seed, reddish foam, history.

I'M READING YOUR MIND

here. Have been for centuries. No, longer. Everything already has
been. It's not a reasonable place, this continuum between us, and yet
here again I put the olive trees in, turn the whole hill-sweeping grove down, its
mile-long headfuls of leaves upswept so the whole valley shivers its windy silvers,

watery…A strange heat is upon us. Again. That was you thinking that. I *suggested* it.
Maybe the wind did. We both put in the horizon-line now, the great loneliness, its
grip, chaos recessed but still there. *After finitude you shall keep coming towards me* it
whines, whitish with non-disappearance. We feel the same about this. The same

what? We feel the *is-there-more*. That's the default. We want to live with the unknown
in front of us. Receding, always receding. A vanishing moving over it all. A sleepy
vacancy. It's the sky, yes, but also this thinking. As from the start, again, here I am,
a mind alone in the fields, the sheep riding and falling the slants of earth, the

drowsiness a no-good god come to assume we are halfwits, tending, sleepy, these
animals gurgling and trampling, thistle-choked, stinging. A dove on a stone. No sky
to speak of. And the god lingers, wants to retire, thinks this is endgame. What
could we be—mist about to dry off, light about to wipe a wall for no reason, that

random? This must have been way BC. Or is it 1944. Surely in 2044 we shall be
standing in the field again, tending, waiting to surprise this god who thinks he knows
what he's made. Well no. He does not know. We might be a small cavity but it
guards a vast hungry—how bad does *that* hurt you, fancy maker—you have no idea

what we turned our backs on to come be in this field of earth and tend—yes tend—
these flocks of minutes, whispering till the timelessness in us is wrung dry and we
are heavied with endgame. Have I mentioned the soul. How we know you hustled
that in, staining this flesh with it, rubbing and swirling it all over inside with

your god-cloth. Rinse. Repeat. Get this—here with this staff which soon I shall turn
into a pen again—brilliantly negligent, diligent, inside all this self truly formless—I
hear the laughter of the irrigation ditch I've made, I see the dry field blonde-up and
green, day smacks its lips—& they are back, the inventors, they are going to do it

again, sprinkle-seed, joker-rain coming to loosen it all. How many lives will we be
given, how many will we trade in for this one—it comes in bushels, grams, inches, notes,
crows watch over it all as they always have, come back from the end of time to caw
it into its redo again. Cherish us. We will not stop. Nothing to show for it but doing. The

flock runs across as the dog chases and I walk slowly. I admire what I own, what I am,
and I think the night is nothing, the stars click their ascent, & I feel it rise in me, the
word, I feel the skull beneath this skin, I feel the skin slick and shine and hide
the skull, and it is from there that it rises now, I taste it before I say it, this song.

MY SKIN IS

parched, on tight, questioned, invisible, full of so much evolution, now the moment is
gone, begin again, my skin, here, my limit of the visible me, I touch it now, is
spirit-filled, naturally-selected, caught in the storm here under this tree, propped up by
history, *which*, I don't know which, be careful, you can't love everyone—

brought to you by Revlon, melancholy, mother's mother, the pain of others,
spooky up close in this mirror here, magnified to the 100th, brutal no-color color,
what shall I call it, shall I pass, meandering among the humans, among their
centuries, no safe haven this *as if*, this spandex over a void, no exception, god

watching though casually, paring, paring, a glance once in a while—what am I
missing—what am I supposed to do now suddenly, what at the last minute here—
what is there to fix—are we alone—am I—packaged so firmly for this short
interval—vigorous skin, doomed outsideness of me—sadder & no wiser here,

blown up, so close, so *only here*, I see you net that skeins me in, tight inside my
inwardness—at *this* border judged—at *this* edge bleeding when hit—as was for a
while—didn't know enough to leave—didn't see the farewell—right there in front of
me—must it always end this way—must I ceaselessly be me, reinvent you, see the

artifice *us*, feel hand-to-face the childhood gone, the starlight the wind the gaze the
race, the stranger not knowing, the unsaid unsaid, unseen unfound—look how full of
void it is this capture, this skin no one can clean, and thoughts right there
beneath—of course you cannot see me for this wrapping—I notice the cover of *your*

face, the dress *you* hide beneath, you sitting there, reading me—pay mind, pay it
out, peering as we are at each other here—dermal-papilla pigment-layer
nerve-fiber blood and lymph, can we still fit into this strictest time, so quick, one click and
hurry up—we've been trying forever now to get out of this lonely place—inside's inside—

the movie of the outside was all about exploring, we explored, we found what we
should never touch, we touched, we touch, what's so unusual we say, you are now
mine we say, this is the feature coming on, this future, so full of liking & fine dis-
closure, a bud-tip pushing aside its sheath, then standing there, very whole now, very

official, open to damp, heat, stippling, shadow—to freckle, slap, beauty or no
beauty—please help me here as I can't tell—the trees don't know—the wind
won't speak—the gods should but their names are being withheld—because some of us
are murdered, and some of us have mouths that keep saying yes, do that to me

again, I know it hurts but yes, I am an American, I like it harder than you'll ever
know, this is Tuesday, the day rises with its fist over the harbor saying give it to me
and the day obliges, saying more, more, do you want more, and the torch of dawn
says more, yes more, ask for my identification, my little pool of identification, here

on the only road, arrested again among the monuments.

WHEN OVERFULL OF PAIN I

lie down on this floor, unnotice, try to recall, stir a little but not in heart, feel rust coming, grass going, if I had an idea this time, if I could believe in the cultivation, just piece it together, the fields the sky the wetness in the right spot, it will recline the earth it does not need your map, the rows you cut into it make their

puzzled argument again, then seed, Spring has a look in its eye you should not trust anymore, just look at it watching you from its ditch, its perch, heavy on the limbs, not reproach exactly not humor though it could be sly this one who will outlive you of course, this one who will cost you everything, yes, sly—do you catch my meaning

says the cosmos-laden morning, I will cover you with weeds, I will move towards beginning but I will not begin again, the marsh gleams does it not, the two adolescent girls walking through it now, in the reprieve, they remind you, do they not, a summer frock underneath, a heavy coat over, so ready, the idea of a century

being *new* beckoning, this one will end, that one we will traverse into via small bomb perhaps, and the marsh waits, speckling, unremarkable, but yet you want to remark it, even by looking away you want to keep it normal, normal you say, rust can you be normal in me, marsh with your rusty grasses come, bring it again my

normal, a bit frostbitten at the start of the day, but now warming where the horizon blues, where the wren has alighted right here camouflaged in normalcy, he left one feather on the ground, I'll bend to pick it up after he goes, it too is all wings the day, it flaps its brightness on and the fields flatten, the sun lies oily in the sillion, furrow-

slice, mold. Are you with me. It's not a good idea this one. The assembly lines, the jet trails, the idea of prayer, thievery, scaffolds, money, how quickly they all vanished. The new thing now is not going to be new by the time you read this. And even as I look at it, trying to feel the seed pushed in, the brimming of those shoots, the eyes of the hare in the ditch pecked out, the horse standing in the field whose breath is plume—gaze after gaze I look at this foreign country, which was so ready, which fell ill so suddenly. We were driving along in one century, we took a back road, it was allowed, there was a herd of goats, we got out to see, they came up to us making

sounds like Latin, they were thin, grey, caked legs with seaweed hair. We looked at each other. Gradually something passed from one creature to the other. Which one was I. I want this normal again. Did I remember just now that this all disappeared. I lie on this floor. I feel the wide slats of the old-growth pine along my back. They

push up into my gravity, I think, I push my place down into place, eyes closed I push down through the subflooring the foundation into grey soil not touched by light in centuries. I'll break it open now. I'll push into the roots that died when place was cleared of place. Dismembered roots, here was my zip, my street address. My name.

OVERHEARD IN THE HERD

You have to make sure you have skin in the game was one of the rules they
yelled out near the end. Also one must *have hope*. Also *watch the clock, the clock is
running out*. Out of what. I had hoped to escape. To form one lucid unassailable
thought. About what? It did not matter *about what*. It just needs to be, to be

shapely and true. Let me tell you. To feel a thought one came up with one's self.
Out of one's *interiority*. There. That's the whole story. If humanity. If to hang on claw
back what to call it. However atrophied. Not *not-living*. Yes horribly close-
quartered. However much we missed the bus. However much we should have

been there while it lasted. Hear us: it lasted. Even here off the bus its lastingness
keeps blossoming & spooling onward. Yes *it's a game it's always just a game*. The wind is
hissing this all afternoon. But even it, raspy and weakening, plunders this space that it
might find some emptiness. *From mind*. Lean in & you'll hear plenitude. Listen it's trying

to make a void again. In which to hear itself. It's too alone. Everything wants em-
bodiment. But there's this noise now it's replacing everything. This humming of agreement
fast-track skipped-step information yes yes yes yes lost hope lost will—dear dis-
embodiment, here is an old wind, watch it orchestrate event, I raise my hand to find

my face again, I know I am supposed to think I'm whole, there is no holiness in me,
can I begin again, I'd like to try to get this right, we might if gotten right go
on, whom am I speaking to, whom, I'll pick up the acid the wrappers the 3D glasses, I'll
gather up the spotless tools printers magnifiers, the place is wired for sound I'll cut

the wires, I'll drag the cursors off, I'll sweep it clean, they've taught me to, I think this way
because I am human, that's my secret occupation, I am unusually common, I can get it
right if you just tell me, we have a shot, whom am I speaking to, why is that laughter
seeping-out nonstop from the invisible, from hospice hospital embassy cathedral—

oh ghost institutions—why must you hover here—spy here—before me always though invisible. Or is it invincible. I can't make out the words being said. Or is it sent. In my direction. I'll wait for an answer. I have indeed nothing better to do. I have nothing actually at all to do. We cannot remember having that—a thing to *do*. To *be needed*

what was that like. To figure, discover, uncover, recover. To make bring think shape. To fold, to crease prepare serve-up. To imagine. To buy hold name sell. To shape. To order. This haunts us now. To make a thing for another. For another's use. To fashion, to offer, to bring, hide, make. To serve. Oh to serve….My new humanity is now relieved of

duty. My soul has its alarm turned off. No my soul has this knot in its throat—or is it a gag—pacified, petrified, up all night counting silently towards infinity. Losing its place. How many of us are left. What else could happen. Has it all already happened. Who is they. That autocorrected to *thy*. Why. No matter what I say it fixes it. It's fixed.

[TO] THE LAST [BE] HUMAN

Today I am getting my instructions.
I am getting them from something holy.
A tall thing in a nest.
In a clearing.
There is a little dread no memory and everything's looking for
signs. We don't know
if this is the way forward or the way
back. Do you? Is it a hundred yards or a million years. A small conifer
appears to be laughing.
Wind would be nice but
it's only us shaking.
Listen up it says. Loosen up. It's all going to be
ok. Going to be fine. Give me your hand. What is this you
are giving me, where are
your hands, what can you
grip. The thing I am asking for, it is not made of
words. No. It is not made of
data. No.
Let's get the map I say. Let's
browse through. Over here famine over here
switchbacks over here to the best of my recollection haunted
faces of those on
the road. The road itself moving as if in a
molten fury. One of us had come back from some other place—
Alaska, a father dying in rage, screaming on his
floor, saved by
nothing.
We're so full of the dead the burnt fronds
hum, getting going each day again into too much sun to no
avail. I was human. I would have liked to speak of
that. But not now. Now is more

complicated. I have no enemy except day. The edges
turn hot and
stay
hot. Shadow hard to find and those threads of it
like hoarded rations. Temp dies down only
slightly but it is
everything, lungs tight as fists inside, yr name just about stripped from
u if u try to say it out
loud, fetuses like flames going out as they
arrive. Someone found a light bulb in a spot where mud still
was. It looks more alive than we had
recalled. We imagine what it
might seem like
lit. A palpitation of light strokes our imaginations. We are never sure
what was memory, sweet, burning, gigantic, silent—
long erasure underneath the
wind—which comes by so in-
frequently we all stop when it
arrives.
You remember u understood completely *that u are lost.*
The phone call comes. You pick up the
receiver and hear the
final sounds of the islands. They are murmuring we want to
weep and lie down. They lie down. Voice lies
down. Says hello
in the normal way. So it all seems like
the world as it had always been, has always been. Here in the
sliver-end of the interglacial
lull. Human time. It
seems.
Then the voice says it's not good
news. From now on you are alone. Whatever *before* had meant

before, now there is a blister over time. Savor of the up-
ahead—lovely blown dust at yr footsteps—gone.
So one has to figure out now how to
understand
time. Your time & then
time. Planet time and then yr
protocols, accords, tipping points,
markers. Each has a prognosis. Each has
odds. You stop on the bridge in the evening on your way
home and look down to see the
empty riverbed
flow. In you
the minutes flow.
The idea is to feel them?
What are our rates of speed. Where is runaway. How far
away. I listen for it.
The city sounds. The sockets of
my eyes. I feel them. The dust
that will cover it all. The sky peered into when I am gone by
others.
Will the river fill again.
Will there be pity taken.
Will it ever rain again.
What is *ever*. What is *again*.
What is it we mean by
ok. Take this October. The deep white turn the air is taking.
How many more
Octobers. Is there another October with us in it.
Blood flows in my hand writing this.
The crows glance through the upper branches.
They are not waiting.

FROM THE TRANSIENCE

May I help you. No. In the mirror? No. Look there is still majesty, increase, sacrifice. Night in the flat pond. Moon in it/on it disposing entirely of mind. No. Look there is desert where there was grassland there is sun-inundation like a scrupulous meditation no message just mutter of immensity where it leaks into

partiality. Into you/me. Our boundaries now in the epic see-through, how they elude wholeness, let in illusion, pastness, whole years in a flash, then minutes that do not end—that desert—that jungle. No you say, no world, swamp, reeds, grassy shapes, beginning of endings, no you say staring right back at event—it keeps

turning—no that will not be the shape I am/it is/again—it just *was*—the *shape* it was was never the shape it was—sharpness is melding into blur—used to be the sublime— used to be present tense—seat of the now-dissolved *now.* No. My self, my one *one- self* isn't working for me. *I* flaps its empty sleeves. Habit stares at the four

horsemen from the end's endlessly festooned terrace. It stares. Bullets whine. *I* dreams of being a girl, a man, of wearing hooves, of being just sweat and whinnying, *I* smears itself with hope fear disorder opinion, leaves a trail of—what is it of—a smear of beginning, of circles about to close, the manes are tossing in the

light. No. Do not trust what I see. Do not trust you. Do not trust my own saying of the not trust. Do not trust world, the no-place into which I place my *no,* the *state of mind* into which I must clamp my mind, these objects which do not exist, no do not, in the actual, which *depart from* reality. *Swim against current* my opacity my soul whirs,

swim hard against the current state of….May I touch the place that is you. No. Would you have had a place once. Yes. Is there a present tense now. No. What is there? *Touch it.* This place where we share this mind. It will be our first and last. Our first and last *what?* Our first and last. Did we live among men. Were we mouth-

pieces. Where is the mask that worked so well. The carnival. The puppetmaster who
held my strings—my strings—here was my arm as it reached out a hand to you, to
express love, to rid itself of love—here was my mouth in which breathing forced
awake the unending sounds, of blood, of ink, so each made of himself a net,

a grip upon place. Such as this present I can summon here with you. *Here.*
Now, remember that. I see you nowhere, I hear you nowhere, we are
on different pages, not a different story, the ancestor the divided cell keeps
asking have you heard the nightingale—no—have not—listening now is

few and far between—mostly it is more opaque—not talk, not thought, but
like it. But you are still standing there. So very bright, my past. Hello. Dear fission,
my self isn't working for me. It's involved with arithmetic. It's trying to correct itself so that
it fits, to slice itself, dismember, un-remember, cut off, sew on, recall until it can be

counted on, or in, or up, or down. It says some right fit must be found—restored resolved
bought-up doomed-to—it must be worn more artlessly the new thing they will call
the self—we must not make the same mistake again—what was it was mistaken ask
the vigorous winds, bending down gently as if to lift us up, right through our throats

as fish used to be hooked when there were fish—for nothing is more important than
this new face that must shake the whole thing down & laugh & bring-up the rear.
What time is it. Are we already in the necroscape. Even as a machine I recall
the dust and ash which everyone assured everyone else was just a small digression.

PRAYER FOUND UNDER FLOORBOARD

Listen. We are crowds now. We gather in the eardrum of.
The scaffolding grows.
As if the solution.
There is not a soft part of us.
Except for the days in us.
We let the pieces fall where they may.
The visible in its shell gets smashed.
The desperation re
the gorgeous raw material—earth—the sensation of
last night, storms spilled, plumed, odor of
looking for the various directions
though it makes no difference.
I have seen
nothing. It is deafening. It shakes with laughter
with ways of looking. It rattles. Listen. How much is it now
the thing I want?
The soft wind is it recompense?
But I was trying to tell you about us now.
How we finally realized we made no difference.
And the visible we love. Its notes its intervals.
Over which the sunlight still proceeds shivering with precision.
With the obligation of precision.
The visible whose carapace we love.
And how our love is *that we are seen*.
All the way into
the mind *are seen*.
The earth with its fingers in our mouth nose ears.
The visible with its ghosts its smooth utmosts.
And weight and limit—how they heave
up—pray for us we are destroyers—
pray we fail—the mind must fail—
but still for now a while longer let me

who am part of it & must fail & the pieces
which must not *fall where they may*,
they must not, as all is hearing this
from the deep future, deep origin….cry.
Cry mind sick with the delight of getting it always only right.
Cry fingering the earth every crevice.
Cry all the trees like a problem you
can solve.
How could you not have maintained steady state.
It is lean this unfolding of
your days over this earth. Listen, a flap
where a gate shuts, where the next step is
coldly placed without hope—& crackles
rising where your footfall goes—oh
I am huge—I would
take back names give up the
weight of being give up place
delete *there* delete *possess*, go,
love, notice, shape, drift, to be in minutes once again, in just one hour
again. Look
my small hand comes out of my pocket
asking to *touch* one more time. Without
taking. To touch. To not take away
any sensation any memory. To come to
the feeling-about at the edge of the object
and stay. Release focus. Release shape.
If we
back off release blind ourselves thumb away hope…
But I am huge.

CARNATION/RE-IN

I am down to my food. I root and divide. I am not pushed down I push. I with my
mouth use my nose where are my hands. I say who am who am I
now. I ask what color am I now. I try to feel my skin but my head is fixed to my
food and my hands where are my hands. What skin am I I ask. You have no skin

they say. You are wrapped don't worry you won't fall out. It's a new material. Am I
alive. Of course you are. You are always going to be alive. If I could just turn and
look at my self. Do I have a self where are my hands but then feel fingers and
they are tucked in. We used to have skins. Do I have the other parts. Am I

on my knees. I must be pretty normal I think. Am I normal I ask. Human? I talk to
you you answer me are we speaking *what* are we speaking. Are these words
actually being pronounced. I remember. I remember we were overfull of
pain. The house went under the mud. It was an avalanche it went under but not

into the earth. Now now is everything. Near the top they are still looking for
bodies. Deep under some other *people* will find books. They will find my pills and
shoes. I imagine my red shoe being found "when the geology thinned earth again"
and up it shoved into history, & my nightstand, & the towel I had just put down, &

the bronze buddha from that world, the kitchen pots, my teacup was just full
of tea. Before that fire came. We burned but enough survived that we had to go on
living. Now that there is nothing now. Now that if. Look back you see a continent
of _____. Where there had been. I went forward on this piece of time. Called it a

road. Tried to feel my step. There is some kind of movement I am making. *Into
forward* I remember thinking. I remember thinking. This is a narrow place. Is it
now. Try to feel if you have footing. A tightrope of feel/no feel. There is sun it
seems, I am high up in the burned no-root-life, I net it in place, we left place under

the avalanche, five inches in five minutes I remember *came down*, down is where, what is *up*. But I can still see the mountain up against the sky. Where it was supposed to be. What is supposed to be. And the _____ between its peaks. I walk out again looking. I look......out. Sometimes down. At _____. See

below. See the _____ spread out over what we had made of. The earth. Streets houses plots lawns our view each slightly different. Now I am in. The earth. I wade out through it. The earth. My neighbor is under went in a flash. The door flew & she was under. My other neighbor is in the tree. The child ours stayed on

her couch would not come called called called. Here we are told *they* sit there underneath for good. Encased in. The earth. It closes over again now it has taken what was needed in payment desire what am I to do with it yes I feel them my hands but can't won't raise them to look am told to carry myself forward in this

walking forward every where is forward. I remember gravity. Remember place.

BECOMING OTHER

The corpse at the heart of our theorization of us. That turn back to look. Once again. Ignoring the mirror. Baroque turn. Who *are* you. Non-alive. Being's obsession. I'll take your photograph. Are you on holiday. I need a servant. No, I need to be a servant. That is the [only] source of pleasure now. Pleasure now. Neither one thing nor another. Between two fixed states. Decomposing. Pleasure now. Formless as….

Begin again. A substance that does not hold its form. What *up-holds*? Can it be overthrown? No. Delights you to death. Rides the back of time to the mass grave. Takes its time. Spreads like memory or a shade through an afternoon in summer, time itself the detention camp, accident a gleam in the eye of time—one day I was born—that was my important point—my point of view—but you do not *realize* you're an

aperture in time, an asking-for, a decision cast like the spell of a wild die through the *yes/no.* I was a woman. Not as untroubled as I seem. As we seem. As I think. I have interests. It seems to me they are mine. This identity you are listening to, here, is an embarrassment of riches—take my picture, take care of me, take forever, take this in hand, in mind, this emptiness into which we slap a purpose, shuttered against

the eyes of neighbors. Our personhood. So dressed-up this nakedness. Pre-need. Pre-individual. Then post. Under-ripe then overripe before you even feel it slip by. I have to get the pills, the wind comes up, the dazzled memory of having had shiny expectations, no matter, the grass shivered, then the stars, you'll know how to stand, you'll know how to lie with another, you'll feel that new flat solitude. You're free,

aren't you. The signs at the crossroad are pointless. For those trips out of the ghetto I decided not to see that I couldn't see. Unlike the hawk. Drink up. You only have these dregs of sun. The worst has befallen. It won't see you through. Boundlessness came and went and you stood and walked. There was the wasted splendor of day every day. No one looked. Vastness played all over us, slippery, &

slid off like a ring into the sea. We looked through the roiling waters but tide came in fast. Years later in the tub you still run your hand through the fold. Who are you. Nothing in all the directions. A sapphire. Keep groping. The wide open grave awaits the sacrament of your mindless waiting. Imploding last stand of the small human. Voluptuousness of defeat. We are fanatical. What are we supposed to

admit to, possess, name. Far from diminishing the appetite for power, this suffering gorges it. Mind loves it. Renunciation our active ingredient. Our formula for post-animality. The pre-personal pilot of what. *In* what. Row. Row, thermospasm. Be in being for now. Brief progeny. Row. Merrily. Gently. Down. The stream will hold you for now—machinic and hungry. Pre. Post. No. Where? Reflection is very late. Row

in your amniotic sac—hope for mud, slime, mold, dust, running water, flame. Rain.

THAW

There is a plot in the back of my building.
Not the size of the asteroid.
Not what four
hyper-crenellations of a reef would have held when there were
reefs. It's still here. I must not
get the time
confused. The times. There is a coolness in it which would have been new
Spring. I can't tell if it's
smell, as of blossoms which would have been just then
beginning, or of loam. Through this
green sensation is
a thing which threads & pushes
up. What is it pushes it. Whatever pushes it we
must not get the feelings confused, the feelings of this—in this—
now. One of us looks in
the field guide. One of us looks up to where the sky had been.
Our prior lives press on us.
Something with heavy re-
collection in it
presses. Not
history anymore of course but
like it. Is it five minutes or 500 years. Can we pencil that
in. Next to the ashheap. The windowless classroom or what we still call class-
rooms. Out of habit. Which feel, as the monitors speak, like
they're filling with snow. Each creature sits
alone. Is that what it is, a
creature. It feels like a resurrected thing, this sensation I have of a
creature. I carry certain stains with me. I can imagine
loneliness which is an error I know. I think of causes &
effects which is a form of regret. I imagine this veil
shall be lifted again and something like a face in a mirror
appear. And it will be me. Will be a room as rooms used to be to us.

And us in them.
As a family or as lovers. We shall be lifted and we shall touch
in the old way. Just a hand on another. Not meaning that
much but still a small weight. With
meaning. A feeling of a harboring inside which reminds one of having a
mind. A feeling that one could
die for instance.
So there was
mystery, hope, fear, loneliness.
A sudden alarm from not-knowing and being startled by an in-
comprehensible terror or some other reaction
to change. There was
change. A person could be-
come. You could look into a face &
not know. There was rain & you would hardly notice.
It could rain for hours. The face would be there inside
its otherness, the way its body, which you could not imagine the in-
wardness of, moved, each one
moved,
differently, completely
differently. Why is it now you summon
streets. How they ran everywhere away. You could be in a strange
place and not know. You could be
lost. You could be as if
thrown away from the real. A trembling thing. A
journey. Lost yes—but not wrong in being. And from there you
could see a face which was a stranger. And it
would have a look which you had to wait for.
Because it was *its* look.
Because you could not program it or request it.
Because it was not yours.
Not yours.
And when it came your way like a strange turning

it brought a gaze with it. An ex-
pression. A thing given to you you had not made or owned or seen
before.
That's all. You do not know how to go on from here.
You do not know how to imagine further
into the past.
You want to remember what it was to see a look.
There is one look among all the unprogrammable looks you want to recall.
You raise your hands to your face to feel for it, can you force it.
It was like this:
someone turned your way.
It was a free turn. It was made by them freely.
And what they did then was this.
You had done something. You
seemed to become un-
masked. You
had done something you should not have done. You felt in you that u
wished you had not.
And they did something with their free face,
they tossed it out at you,
a thing not yours to dial-up or own—a thing free—a free thing—
they forgave you.
You are not sure you know what this means. But you are sure this happened once. You
were a thing
that required it.
And it was a thing which was not exact, not on time, not wired-in,
which was able to arrive in
time—just in time—& could be
given.

EXCHANGE

You. You at the door a crumpled thing when I open
surprised. *Sing*, you hiss. *Prosecute, sentence*, waving your thin not-arms like a dollar
bill, your bewildering moldy skin—one or two of you are you, are you a god now,
bony, wing-beaten down, smaller than
ever, not dead as you should be but not
alive either as you indicate mumbling almost falling in on
your clawed feet—*I still have desire*—you float—at my
small door—me inside—me inside life. Are you newborn now, I
ask. Are you remnant. Why. *Why are there moneylenders*
you say swatting me away when I ask can I help, growing more
crumbled, but more than just cloth—all feather
burlap, beak, fingergrip, all edge and cling. A thing not
formed or not divided yet. Pre-conception. Just at the threshold. Almost falling in your
uneven crouching. Your chest a pulsation. A languishment that will not

die. What is *die*. Now there is not blood on the earth
anymore. We disappear. We pixilate. Races or places, is it.
Which? Remember what it was to carry your load? Your *you*. That
weight. Wondrous it was. At intervals light-struck. Silence and then the
cutting of water, sleeping audible, thrown about by breath, keeping a sharp lookout—
here's where free choice vanished, here rights, here the
real meaning of the word—(you choose)—consequence, capital, commodity, con-
sumption. Community? *Come here* says time. Just try to
find it, the *here*. Such a good game to keep you
occupied for now. The rest of the now. It's going to be a long
time. Why are you here. *What are they lending you.*
How can it be loaned. What is a loan. The changers.
Who gets to keep it. No one gets to keep it. No one. None of it.
What is *it*. The money changers. What can
you change *it* into. What else do you
want the *things* to become. But it won't stay still as

currency either. It will be changed again.
Shape-shifting and all the other tiny adjustments. Currency
manipulation—feel it—all those other
hands on it, each with its own need, having
held it—grasped, changed, folded, tucked, handed—oh
look it becomes virtual—the fingerprint is lifted off,
its little stain—no one's need is on it any-
more. It's clean. It has never been, and never again
will be, touched. The looping ledger of the fingerprint's
wish. I signed my name to this. *Did you*. In the hush. At the center.
Among the closed shutters at the height of the day I
signed. I clenched the pen and then my dream. It flowed. No one is

ever at home. I don't know why. Had been told to live by any means
possible. Did. Beyond, the sea. You could feel this period coming to
an end. All of it. A bomb went off, legs went off, means went
off, blew off, like gossamer—nothing stalled—you couldn't get it to
stall—seemed painted-on but it was not, was sleeping, reality finally was
sleeping—so deeply—you couldn't wake it up again, you couldn't
wake yourself again—it rained—time sputtered now and then like a regurgitation
of space. It's a jail, light says, but it looks like just being
lost, full of the things we needed to learn, us ready to step up and offer
our lungs, intake and out, *change me* we say. We want to be
identified, written-in, collected. Worth me up. Give me my true
                                        value…
But still I have to bring this to you in these

words, cracked glaze all over it, little holes over it, belief drilled through,
self, that boutique, gone under, such dark windows, history arrested….
History arrested. How is that possible. It flowed. It flowed without us, us on it if we

could catch a ride sometimes. How do you live in this end. I look at you. You have been
through. Your war is done. I try to squint it in. Do you really want to
begin again. Is that why you're here. I feel I could count your
fingers, each hair left on you, each thread of skin, each crease. Four or five times you
cast a glance on us. But then it's done. Your passing by us now a
buzzing of flies. You stand at the window and the song begins. We don't know
what to do with it, the moon, that monster, the fame and the thirst,
the night out there a shirt rolled up to reveal what dusk had
hid—a murky heart, a love that would never be replaced.
But they are still there on the steps—the money changers. The steps
of evening rise. They want you to exchange. That is the sacrament. Why does he
                                                keep throwing them out.
Day after day. Forever. Listen to me, you say, you are going off into
thought, it is not a real road. Take yourself

off the road. He is and is not but he is. And
you are always in the holy place. Because
just being in it makes it holy. Uphold it. Linger. Be eternal for this
instant. Lodge in. I cannot say *in what*. Have spent a lifetime saying *in*. In flow,
in promise, rich, in haste experiment crowd season in bias gnawing at
hope invisible in time standing in it confounded tongue in my mouth about to
curl up, speak, promise, taste promise, laugh at the ignorance, cherish
ignorance—don't leave—this is where I've arrived—don't
slip away, the reverse of the watching and waiting is finally here, wasn't mine, wasn't

me speaking either. Not anymore. This is that dream. The darling of
failure. No identification. All impending and then the *now* strikes. It is
unbreakable. It is. You must believe me. I want to be here and also there where you
receive this but I can't. That's the whole story. I will never know
what is there to know. You will not be changed. You must believe.

SAM'S DREAM

One day there is no day because there is no day
before, no yesterday, then a now, & *time*, & a cell
divides and you, you are in time, time is in you, as
multiplying now u slip into our stream, or is it u grow
a piece of stream in us, is it flesh or time you grow,
how, is it an American you grow, week 28, when we
are told dreaming begins. Welcome. Truest stranger.
Perhaps one of the last conceived & carried in womb.
Father and mother singular and known. Born of
human body. Not among the perfected ones yet. No. A

mere human, all firsthand knowledge, flying in as if
kindling—*natural*. The last breath before the first
breath is mystery. Then u burn into gaze, thought,
knowledge of oblivion. Rock yourself. Kick so I can
feel you out here. Push your hands against the
chamber. The world is exhausted. I moisten my lips
and try to remember a song. I have to have a song to
sing you from out here. They say you now hear *vividly*.
This could have been a paradise my song begins. No,
this is, was, is, never will be again, will be, we hope

desperately wasn't a dream, maybe in your dream
now there is a clue, can you dream the clue, you who
are dreaming *what* having had no life to dream *of*,
dream *from*—what populates you—bloodflow and
lightswirl, stammering of ventricles, attempts at
motion, absorbings, incompletions, fluidities—do you
have temptation yet, or even the *meanwhile*—such a
mature duration this meanwhile, how it intensifies
this present—or *nevertheless*—no *beyond* of course
in your dream what could be beyond—no

defeat as so far no defeat—cells hum—no *partiality*
as all grows in your first dream which is the dream of
what you are—is that right—no *attempt* as there is
no attempting yet—no *privacy*—I laugh to myself
writing the word—oh look at that word—no
either/or—but yes light filtering-in, root-darknesses,
motion—and the laughter, do you hear it from us out
here, us, can you hear that strain of what we call
sincerity—Oh. Remain unknown. Know no daybreak
ever. Dream of no running from fire, no being shoved

into mass grave others falling over you, dream of no
bot, no capture filter store—no algorithmic memory,
no hope, realism, knowing, no quest-for, selling-of,
accosting violently to have, no lemon-color of the end
of day, no sudden happiness, no *suddenly*. It is much
bigger, faster—try to hear *out*—this place you're
being fired into—*other* in it—*judgment of other*—
logic, representation, nightmare—how to prepare
you—what do you dream—what must I sing—it says
you cry in there & laugh—out here a late October

rain has started down, soon you shall put your small
hand out & one of us will say slowly and outloud *rain*
and you will say *rain*—but what *is* that on your hand
which falling has come round again in the forever of
again to reach your waiting upturned hand. I look up
now. Clouds drift. Evaporation is a thing. That our only
system is awry a thing. That u will see rains such as I
have never seen a thing. Plain sadness, this hand-knit
sweater, old things, maybe u shall have some of—in
this my song—in my long song not telling u about the

paradise, abandoning my song of what's no longer possible, that song, it is a thing. Oh *normalcy*, what a song I would sing you. Child u shall god willing come out into the *being known*. First thing will be *the visible*. That's the first step of our dream, the *dream of here*. You will see motes in light. And lights inside the light which *can go out*. A different dark. And spirits wind exhaustion a heavy thing attached to you—your entity—as u enter history and it—so bright, correct, awake, speaking and crying-out—begins. And all the

rest begins. Amazing, you were not *everything* after all. Out you come into legibility. Difference. *Why shouldn't all be the same thing?* It's a thing, says the stranger nearby, it's a new thing, this stance this skin like spandex closing over you, it's you. A name is given you. Take it. Can you take it? All seems to be so overfull at once. Now here it is proffered again, this sound which is *you*, do u feel the laving of it down all over you, coating you, so transparent you could swear it *is* you, really you, this *Sam*, this crumb of life

which suddenly lengthens the minute as it cleans off something else, something you didn't know was there before, and which, in disappearing now, is felt. The before u. The before. That dream. What was that dream. There, as if a burning-off of mist, gone where— not *back*, where would *back* be—dried away—a sweetness going with it—no?—feel it?—I do—I almost smell it as it is dissolved into *the prior* by *succession*, by events, not raging, not burning, but going—nothing like the loud blood-rush in the invisible u & u in with its elasticities, paddlings, nets, swirls. In this disunion now stretch. Take up space. You are that place u displace. That falling all round u is gazing, thinking, attempted love, exhausted love, everything, or it is everyone, always going and coming back from some place. They do not stay. *They do not stay*. And then out here circumference. One day you glimpse it, the horizon line. You are so....surprised. How could that be. What are we in or on that it stops there but does not ever stop. They tell u try to feel it

turn. The sun they will explain to you. The moon.

How far away it all becomes the more you enter. How

thin you are. How much u have to disappear in order

to become. In order to become human. Become Sam.

SAM'S STANDING

on earth—almost—testing the weight she brings, her *self*, to the
hold earth offers-up—she looks—she holds an edge to see
if space too has grips in it somehow—how is she supposed to
let go and just launch, lurch—*fly out*—& who
will be there where there is no one visible at all in case
there is suddenly nothing at all. One foot is set in place,
feels hard for place, then the whole of her eleven
months leans on it, lets go—is this trust now, first trust—uneven then
even—then the one step. All stops. She looks firmly at the emptiness.
It seems so full. What is it to *go*. Its gorgeousness

has not yet shown itself, this void into which all shall pour
of her self, where she must cut off *here* from *there*—
it is not easy this finding a *there*, an *elsewhere*—is there arrival anywhere—is
there going *around* or *into*—is there thru—what is thru—urgent not to miss
the mark which won't stay marked, this *going* with no *where* in it. Invisibility
is this you. This sudden wanting to be more—to be alone—this fluidity
wanting to rip open where she wasn't before, and pass thru, as if she is
what the thru was, has taken on throughness and is.
In this balancing is. Arms out to the side is. Is just. Feels from earth
this sweet upswirling—coming to hold her—up. Up. *All is equal everywhere.* Birth

continuing until this now, this *forth*, where the perfect calculations of air
hold. And no station is above another. And millions of swerves hum incipient. But for
now stasis—air rushing to hold—her heart aloft—and everywhere the huge bloom
opens—look, it shows its face—*justice*—nothing is missing yet—no *too soon*
too late—found-footing then again found. Ground. Oh ground. Given by
going. Then the stream begins to form. The *where-she's-been*. High
up above the earth—even for so small a thing, so high, *above*, she turns. Sees where
she's been, where she no longer is, will never be again. I see it widen there,
right on her tiny face—the agitation, the vault, the chasm of
minutes opening and brandishing, the dance that begins now, the dance of

terror, I'm seeing it here, I'm watching the minutes open in a soul,
would you like to dance, the generosity of everything murmurs, I see her whole
self hear it, though it is just the air conditioner in here with us, & no it's not
like a photograph of anything this rent—it's not just air she sees—it's not
recoverable—from bed to bed she'll know this—from love to love—the kingdom
of undertow has opened here—*you are expected* it says furnishing from
out of nowhere now the corridor—would you like to dance—outside the winter's
smoothing flat more day, one less, one more of less, though as she enters
now she does not know—I know—I chaos of knowing know—the band
of sunlight moving as she moves into it now, dust motes in it, her hand

thrown out to grab them all. All. It's merely place. It's merely time.
She goes. She has not fallen down so now she is for sure in the human
thoughtlessness, on the conveyor, welcome girl, it's 7:43,
we will never arrive, we will never arrive at mercy,
it is incurable, there is nothing that can be known, just go, tear down
all you have not entered yet and go, your destination
whatever it may be triumphs by being entirely accurate, its calculation
flawless, but for now go, the corridor awaits, your footsteps echo down
its apparent generosity, *do you want to dance* it hums *friend*,
though those are just your bare feet slapping as you feel the accident,

the *feeling* of accident, recede and the feeling of *direction* flow in,
though of course this is not what you thought at all, not then
when you swayed and recovered and felt the high walls flow—they cannot
hold you—nothing can hold you—I see the wilderness of thought
begin in you as you glance up to see where you are going
next. Shall I put a window there for you, a new world. A flowing
day shimmers outside. Here is a wintered tree for you to add now
to the power you feel. I feel the impatience in you being born. How
fast it is, this excited stupefaction, this oblivion, this forgetting of
where you were before, just a minute ago, just a lost minute of

the only time. A crow lands on the tree. He tries to land. He
settles, claws, but the grip slips, he rises up then comes at it again. Be
still. Watch. He's found a spot in winter which is his. His time is not
your time. His gaze casts straight at us where we are watching him. It's hot
with knowing—circles, windrise, drought, sprout, the dip, the
hovering, the dwelling in the hovering. Green black and oily-
black he is. Knows acceleration, prevailing, flow. Erasure of
flow. There is a not-moving in the world. There is a not-moving which
is not a being still. There is this place from which we watch.
There is no way to get to here. There is no way to leave. Love

is the force that made it for you. Here. Don't take your eyes off

him. He'll sit the winter through for you. He's yours. He can't fly off.

WHEREAS I HAD NOT YET IN THIS LIFE SEEN

stillness. Stillness in time. Rich concentrate. Late summer late-day light. Over but
not *on* magenta. *Of.* Of dahlia-heads. Of serrated leaves trimmed gold. Plush stalk
lost-still in non-moment. All awake but no wakefulness. Low. Small. Snug in flooding
light. Unwilled. No speed of anything, no, no motion on surface because suddenly no

surface, all a mechanism yes but now neither on nor off, & shining, & not even a frill
of breeze—as if there had never been time—as if being had never been or not
been—no containing, no cause/effect thing, no, all swallowed by unmovingness of all
things. Grassblades carved still. Leaning-in, angle-of, stalk. Sealed. No flex. Spin. No

rush no struggle no not even the tiniest all unwhirled & stopped till this, what is this,
stands before you, certainty—the pouring of color stopped mid-air—all
outreaching but no towards, lapping, of thing & surround, exquisite, as if eyes closed
though all wide, poured out wide. Try again. Very small the world. Quiet. The

robin's landing on the far lawn heard, lawn heard, as-if heard, strength of the
nothing noticed, not smooth, as if on hold but never again to be released from hold,
shuddering done, no lift or fall, no, no interval, no thought, no whispering of thought,
no. Noticing blends with light. Seeing is light. No trouble in the gaze even as the

gaze gazes upon stillness and is stilled. Where is the motion I know. Where. Any
breeze and I'd be human again. Swirl of leaf and I'd see it again. The vacancy. The
crust afloat above the thing itself. There being no further than this as-if
hallucination. The hallucination of *no as-if*. The end. What is utterly. Is this

ancient. Is this. As if a huge pity but entirely and only made of matter. Where
has motion gone—it has taken time fate need. All lies here now in
the seen. Not seen *as such* just there entire in the laying-out of itself in the
which-is. No *if*. That's it. The stillness of no *if*. Dear friend, you cannot cross here,

this is the visible world, I have seen it in this my life, by accident, just now, I have
recognized it, I do not know that I will glimpse it again in this life, I assume it's my
one life, my mind roves over it all tapping, trying words, again words. The poem
is built for this. To come to this limit & see in & fail. It is built for this particular

failure. This wakefulness that wipes out the waking. This muteness which is the
heart of what. It is not silence. Now each wick is lit as the planet moves into
the end of the visible. The spiderweb is played string by string by the sun. Waits.
Error. Nothing waits. Radical unimagined unreleasable unscatterable unhidden

nothing waits.

RAIL

I set out over the
unknowable earth once
more. Everything
still underfoot. A mat
of fallen and unfallen
matter. Things flinch
but it is my seeing
makes them
flinch. Before, they are
transparent. Now they
line my optic
nerve. I feel them
enter. Brain
flinch husk
groove. Subject.
       Honeysuckle,
       bramble, vine,
       vibration
       and
web-tremble. How
       will the real
       let me drop just
       in time.
How will it pay me
       out,
pass me along to
       the next-on
       I? I
walk down the hill
       where I feel my

letting-go go
        into the down of
        the hill. I
        know I will
        have to leave
        the earth—my
        difference
        looking around
        wildly
        for where it
        ends. That is
        life I say
        humming,
        idling, mind's
        engine dozing
        in me, its
        squint, that
        sweet way of
        inhaling before
        speech while
        the hand slides
        down the spiral
        rail like a
        millennium
        dappled with
        dna and spoor
        just right
        enough to
end.

I WON'T LIVE LONG

enough to see any of the new
dreams the hundreds of new kinds of suffering and weeds birds animals shouldering their
demise without possibility of re-
generation the heart in your tiny chest opening its new unimaginable ways of
opening and to what might it still
open. Will there still be
such opening. Will you dare. I will not be there
to surround you w/the past w/my ways of
knowing—to save
you—shall you be saved—from what—
home from fighting are you, remembering how he or she or they looked at you
while you both fed the machine or built the trough in dirt
where it will be necessary to
plant again—will it open—will the earth open—will the seeds that remain—will you know to
find them in
time—will those who have their lock on you
let the openings which are
chance unknowing loneliness the unrelenting arms of
form, which knows not yet the form
it will in the end
be, open and
form? Will there be islands. Will there be a day where you can afford to think back far
enough to the way we loved you. Words you said
for the first time
as we said them. *Mystery* your grandfather said one day, after saying *shhh* listen to the
birds & you sat so still,
all your being arcing out to hear,
and the bird in its hiding place gave us this future, this moment today when you can recall—
can you—his saying, *there,*
that's a mystery.
And you said the word as if it were new ground to stand on,
you uttered it to stand on it—

mystery. Yes, mystery he said. Yes mystery you said
talking to it now as it
took its step out of the shadow into the clearing and there you
saw it in the so-called in-
visible. Then when the wave broke the first time on what had seemed
terra firma and you knew as he held your hand
insisting you hold your ground
that there was foreclosure,
there was oldness of a kind you couldn't fathom, and there was the terrifying
suddenness of the
now. Your mind felt for it. It felt the reach from an elsewhere and a dip which cannot hold.
Splash went the wave.
Your feet stood fast.
Your hem was touched.
We saw you watch.
We felt your hand grip
but not to move back.
Can you find that now now, wherever you are, even a candle would be a gift I know
from there. *Shhh* he said so you could hear it. *Pity* he said
not knowing to whom.
Pity you said, laughing, *pity pity*, and that was the day of
your being carried out
in spite of your cold, wrapped tight, to see the evening star. And he pointed. And you
looked up. And you took a breath I hear even now as I go
out—the inhalation of dark secrecy fear distance the reach into an almost-touching
of silence, of the thing that has no neighbors and never will, in you,
the center of which is noise,
the outermost a freezing you can travel his arm with your gaze
till it's there. The real. A star. The earth is your
home. No matter what they tell you now and what program you input via your chip or port
or faster yet, no, no, in that now I am not there
in, to point, to take your now large hand and say

look, look through these fronds,
hold your breath,
the deer hiding from the hunter is right here in our field,
it knows we are too,
it does not fear us.
Be still. Wait. And we, we
will be left behind.
Except just now. If you still once.
That you might remember.
Now. Remember now.

SCARCELY THERE

[for J. A.]

After the wind just stops you still hear
the wind's wild *almost*, its approach and retreat, and how it kept on
circling as-if-trying, as if about-to-be, an almost-speech,
loud, full of syntax, casting about for
life, form, limit, fate. To be bodied. To strut. To have
meaning. How easily we wear ourselves
as if it is nothing to have
origin, whirl, outcome,
and still be.
After the high winds stop you're forced to hear
the freshness of what's
there. It smacks, shimmers—this sound of
the scarcely there, this adamantly *almost*, all *betweens*, sub-
siding till adjustment—and then the wide re-blanketing evenness sets in….Gone
all that acceleration, that shooting up & back, futurist, furious with naming and naming
its one price. Oh nothing holds. Just the rattling of the going and
coming together of things, as if matter itself is trying
to find something true to
say—crazed investigation, tentative prophecy, trying on savage
shape—widening without be-
coming—is this the one last war now, finally—but no, only more of notion's
motions—more *more* the wind says, break grief, loosen possibility, let vague
hopes float, sink—let other debris slip into
place. Rootless mind. Shallow whirling of law and more and yet more law
brocading the emptiness. Then suddenly
all stills. It is near
noon. No more
spillage. No more gorgeous waste of effort. No more
out-tossed reachings of green as if imagining some *out there* exists—hovering

inhalations, then as-if-hiding, then all coughed-out at once in a tumble—too much,
too many, disconcerted, un-countable. Yet
no dream....
After the wind stops you hear fact. You hear fact's plan. It is huge.
The tree does not escape. Things are finished forces.
You hear a name-call from far off, tossed, dropped. Someone gives up.
Light rips *here* from *there*. Where birdcalls cease, you hear the under-
neath. *Try living again* day's long pitched syllable-ooze
hums after the high winds stop & your final footprint lifts off & no matter how clean
you want it to be
nothing is ever going to be gone enough. Oh oak, show us up.
Indecipherable-green sound us. Stilled leaf-chatter quiver up
again, rustle the secret rule we'll never catch
in time. To be late
is to be alive. This Sunday. All things *are* mention of
themselves—as the dog barks, the air-conditioner
scours its air—and each thing takes its place. But look,
keenly, adamantly
a road has appeared—a sense that something is *happening* striates
the open air—there is a limping in the light, a tiny withdrawal of light from
light, which
makes a form
in the gully—you haven't changed much it
says—children still appearing out of nowhere now, so violently, heavy with
life—they dart, they breed, *you be the ghost now* the surrounding tunes up,
as if it is all going to begin again, though this time without you
standing here
noticing....So
notice is given. The look on the light
is that of an argument about to be made and won.
Yes you were underneath history for this while,

you were able to write the history of being underneath,
you were able to disappear and make the rest appear.
But now it wants its furious place again, all floral and full of appearance,
its fourth wall, its silvery after-tomorrow,
all ramping-up now quite a spectacular dusk.
This page is turning. It is full of mattering.
Our unrealized project glows in
your mind. The animals lift their heads for an instant
then back. New shoots in the parched field. All the details are important you think but
no, even the ruins look like they might be fake—important but fake—
though we must learn what they have to teach.
This is the way it is something murmurs, circling,
out here, in the middle of summer. Which summer was it was
the last of the summers. All the children are
returned home. Day turns its windless
folio. You stay, it says. We pass here now into the next-on world. You stay.

UN-

blooming mother's fists
tighten daily.
Swipe at bed-
cloth. Jab at

emptiness. Dig
into their own
palms till blood's
drawn & trapped &

no balm will undo the
rot inside. Stiffening
fury. Stony
stunted held up

victorious by the
stringy arm,
up into the humming
room—un-

opening—ready to
strike if u
come near, who had been
so proud of her long-

fingered hands,
holding them out
in front for us
to see—who'd been a

hand model in her
youth—sd this again &
again, finger-
tips pointing thru spring

air with tip of
cigarette for
anecdote &
vodka—once w/

onyx holder
punctuating every-
thing—smiling,
carnelian nails unhooking the

veil over the un-

transcendent—let it
rip—& there, look there, see the curve
shudder in the ripple
Michelangelo makes

right there—extended in-
dication—though all so
swift—gone now—*look*
there—the opposite of

sorrow—*look*—even the angry descent of
those hands in rage
upon me alive w/in-
vestigation—*hurry*—evening

falls, look there, see it light
the far
limb, squint, do not be
visionless—touch it—*something*

might be there—

something not able to get
away—trapped—spiraling—
oh
clenched

clubs to which life
shall be
reduced
now

summoning us with stumps—
farewell to
touch—mother—
who loved yr hands

most of any body

part, who loved yr

self little but so loved

touch—the surface a score you knew to scrawl mold bend, knew to

rip into—what
were u looking to re-
lease—tentacular furious careful—also
tapping—also pressing gently to feel for

edge—loved steel stone wood iron wax melt of
acetylene till yr glove
burned through bc u
cld not wait

to feel the ridges the immanence the shudder of

limit—of
self—loved
punctuating everything w/
a wave. And laugh. What

is laughter
now, strange thing this
new body
won't do. The wind goes over us.

It says what it says.
It does not say why.
Sometimes the earth says
break down shake free bend bend but that

is wind in it
trying to convince
us there are many
ways of seeing

things. There are not.

IV

THE HIDDENNESS OF THE WORLD

The lovers disappear into the woods again. The war is
on. The blizzard on, in its own way. Also many interpretations
on their way—of fascism, of transcendence, of what you mean by
perhaps when you look at me that way. A minute more and then a

minute more you look. And then? And then—everything would have been
different. But the lovers are in the woods again, the signifier is in
the woods, the revolution of the ploughshare in, clod-crumble in, cloud-
tumble, hope and its stumble in—everything would have been, could

have been different—do you not think—and the war still on—and
would you have gone—could you spare an arm, an eye, a foot is a thing
one hopes to keep, one's stop and go, one's step, one's only way
which could have been another way, but wasn't. Do I have to end

in order to begin, I ask the light that lingers on the trees—between the
trees—the lovers have disappeared into again. I cannot breathe. This verge
is taking up all of my life—is it my time or space, I cannot tell—this being here but then
not here, trying to suss out all the fundamental laws—like sniffing-in the day I

think—the human laws, the commonalities we call our word-to-word thing, our
love—what else shall I think—that emotions have no significance? life no validity?
We're going to see a movie later on. There is a terrible thing inside of me.
It must not grow. I can hear my own scared space apologizing now to every

thing. Like a lightning bolt come when a blizzard was expected. It looks
expensive in the sky. Breaks nothing but still whacks us like a stick,
hissing you must forget organic life, your little dagger of right/
wrong, your leprosy of love, of hate, of all such local temporary wonders. The lovers

are taking their time I think. The storm appears above the woods like a radio
left on in an abandoned car. Are they apologizing now, again, to the earth,
are they wishing they could stop and hide—let's be the lucky ones that don't
go out again—are they standing terrified in their Jerusalem of knowing things, of

things, a couple of lucky ducks, blood flowing normally though maybe a little
fast, because of all the promises that must be made, so fast, my arm, my name,
I swear I'll never tell, all the impending before the ambulance of the outside
arrives to touch them when the last trees are surpassed and nothing but

this clearing's left. The light is hammering down its thousand
fists. From war it looks like blossoming. It's forcing the green fuse. It's synthesizing
lapse. The huge wild oleanders sway. It all awaits this temporary race—run
run—our race—the great fires seeping deep into this thinnest moment from the

only now—why don't they wake us—no—we want to sleep—the lovers in the
movie of the woods, I see them from my inner life, I see skin slip, light reach, face scar
itself with time, hair burn, leaf throne itself, and *nothing* turn, brush, sweat—the fire,
the *now*—it screams at us year after year—each day so sweet—almost a

duplicate, unnerving us, celestial us, looking everywhere in day for the origins of,
the hidden part of, the natural—wrong search—wrong fires—nothing will be done in
time—no one wishes to *become*—preparedness is dull—such thirst for this delay,
this looking away, this sanity—the lovers in the woods, really *in* the outside now—un-

bounded delirium, abstraction, hidden real, dark realm—have no more access to

the day....But could it be more beautiful. The wind has dropped. Two cardinals play
in the young oak. They slip and rise. In distance, bells. Wind then no wind. A previous
life, a hummingbird, has found the agapanthus there. It always does. Its blossom
always blossoms just in time. Either nothing is alone. Or everything. You are alone in

the alone. To exit the human is to exit the singular, the plural, the collective, the
dream. The woods have an entrance. From where I watch I do not think I'll see them
exit who went in, here at the start, the only start, we are filtering them out, are leaving them
in dark, in hiddenness, all excess, all sincerity. Don't touch. In the

flamboyant interim, burn. Feel this outsideness here. Here on this page. Here in my head.
You. You in me in this final time. My shadow. Haunted. Organic. Temporary.

[after Edward Thomas]

RUNAWAY

You wanted to
have vision
but the gods

changed.
You wanted to feel
the fraction of the

degree of
temperature
enter the

water, feel the
minute leave the
minutes

behind.
Why not be
happy. What are

they doing
to the minutes.
Each one takes

that minute of you
away. Takes away
hope. We stand

around, we have the
sensation we
dreamed the whole

thing up, we
didn't, & all
around us how alive

rot is, & damp that
never ceases kissing
everything in-

discriminately—yr
hands, yr skin fixed to
fit everywhere tight,

yr lids holding yr
gaze, the rubble, the
anti-microbial skins,

the layers of cello-
phane, the rare &
treasured paper

sack, everything
delivered up to us
as if spectacular, as if

an emergency of the
spectacular,
& new data-sets showing

more new hours days debt melt
faster rising than
ever anticipated,

also those fleeing
told no no, not you, you
are not allowed, where

are yr papers—oh
those—we know we
gave them to u but

here u see we
change our mind—look,
here is a changed

mind, a mind whose house
burned, here is
melted chromium & ash

where yr life was—stay
calm, listen to
authorities, re-

build, imitate, believe,
wait, b/c it will come again,
over the ridge, the

licking flare, as if
pure hunger, or
curling all over u now

the fire of the
flashlight, don't move,
I beg u, never

move, figure out
what the *they* is,
what the *they* wants—

pretend it's laughter, it's a
refrain—*pay up*—as for the
recent past

it's got too much history
a mind can
set the match to—but see, the fire

prefers not to die, no,
& we oblige, we feed it, we
keep it

unpayable.

IT CANNOT BE

undone. As here these words cannot be taken back into the windless wide
unsaid. No. These changes to the living skin of silence, there where your dis-
appearance into nonlife, into no-longer-ever-again-in-life—no—no longer in
creation, no, no more of your kind—changes silence to what can I call it—ex-

tinction—expiration—this new forever—the small boy on the boat in the dark says—says I
was holding you when we got on the boat in the deep night—says I can still feel
you now I feel you—others are pressed against me but this weight in the dark it is
you—I feel for your legs your feet—are you you or are these the pressings of

others—others are not me—once in a while a flashlight but so brief we cannot
be seen. Then it occurs. It cannot be. And *never again* arrives—is it for you or
me it arrives—the moment that cannot be undone. And we are no longer ever again in life
together. Mother. I need you. I cannot be taken back now into the unmade, un-

conceived, unborn, back. You. As here these words in the world you left behind. It's not
the world exactly, now. It is the now. That new world. *Now.* My body keeps living here
under my mind, slackened by thirst. I see light flick and I say to the air I still have
you. I have surfaces and wandering. Like a root always becoming more by going

on. The blackbird in the thicket understands me I think. It shoots through vacancy & knows
all is down to size, direction, speed. I could not find you, I wrestled the men who thought
to rescue me, me who am dead now, I said where is my mother to death which is this
wave, alive, contagious, & scent of brine, & seagulls slicing and feeding—such a soaring

machine. I spent with her a night my hand too tiny for her to find I think though I
touched and touched hoping day would take me into its teeth, interrupt this glassy
hammering of voice and sea, we are mangled, heaps, there are so many ways to be
afraid, it's all right, we were locked together in years, if we don't land again let's not

land again. But don't leave me. I am a work in the turning galaxy at the bottom of
this dinghy, I am a word that cannot be taken back, I want a home, how many inches is
a home, the gulls pull the day aside so I can see, I need a place to be, please not this
camp, this film of sand on me, the dry day's lip, everywhere tin's shadow-splash across my

only face....Abundance where are you. An inch is enough. Moon and a vacant field
with no fear. Normal chimneys with morning-smoke. Water. Enough water. The shape of
water as it falls. Into my hands. To have a bucket of my own. To watch a long time the
water & feel there is always more. To not be afraid of sun. Of wind. My fingers remember,

I wish they would forget. I put them in the water that is not here. I can put them in that
water. It is a special kind. I have imagined it. Therefore it lies so still upon reality. It cannot
be undone, this water without a voice screaming to me of morning arriving
gradually and sharply, as if a fever lifting, dawn like a hand on my forehead saying the

fever broke, today will be a different day than yesterday, the cloth damp now over my
eyes, day is the simplest phrase, I can hear outside the unevenness of the stones, it is our
village again, light spliced by the cries of birds at dawn, I can hear the sand on the
road heading off towards the village, hear oranges pressing against their skins in their still-

living trees, hiss of morning coming on, I have not imagined it, it's day, we have not left yet,
it is not yet decided, drought touches the side of our house, shade is the simplest phrase,
a goat brays in the distance, which is not too far, then wind, the simplest phrase, it has not
said we have to flee, the froth of the goats' milk into the bucket is whispering the

simplest phrase, the broken surface of the well, where the wheel turns, the bucket rakes,
I hear it land, I should not have been afraid, I was not afraid, there was no
fear, ancient toughness lined it all, we were submerged in time not history, you take
your hand off my eyes and lift the cloth. The cool is good. It cannot be undone, it

cannot be unsaid unmade unthought unknown unrecognized untrued. Until it can.

WHOM ARE YOU

speaking to. What is that listening to
us. I'd like to know whom to address. In this we call
the physical world. Is there another where the footfalls go
from this stony path as it grows granular. They dis-

appear. The silence is ruinous. It seems there could be thunder hidden in this blazing
blue, but it's just dry wind reaching the field. I'd like to know again whom to
address. To say warm mist used to arrive in time & settle-in over our summer day. To say
it stayed. It stayed. I say to you *it's summer now* but we don't really know, in the

unlistable new seasons, what this one now is going to be. It's not the one
it was before, last time we called it this, called it *ours*, called it *time*, felt rise in us *hello my
day*, you are all forward now as I stand up in you, and just behind me there
is where you were just now—*just now* we say rising from death again. Would like

to say again *to whom do they go* the curling of these words into this most
immense slow time, this which is summer, was summer, all hum
at zenith, though no clear zenith, no, it all just stays, it flows, it sluices round
the sheep in the near field braying into day's seeping end. Just one. Then one. I hear

them low. I feel the ancient sound come thru the dry late summer air
to me. They do not sing. They say they know. They make one note, only one
note, they say they know they're bred for slaughter, that slaughter is different
from death, also from sacrifice. Would like to know, please, you wood-doves so

alone above the propositions and promises of grass, whom we
address with these slow voices, now raised, now
low. Whatever is proper for this occasion, we find it in us, always ready there
at lip, at sill—the love, the silly alphabet—& here it is again wanting so hard to hold

its world—a shore a sound a form, what whitens the roof as it passes
away—the high thing in us which wishes so for something higher yet—& how it rises now
as if to leap from flesh but not to let it go—rises to drag the body up into the im-
material, knowing each thing to be the ending that it is, wanting to be a wind in wind

as the end of day upwells→is it bad to have come here→to have come by this route—
is it good to have come at all→was this the only way we came even if it's not the way we
should have come—there won't be more of our supremely simple being—no—will not—
as dusk picks up each needle of the pines against last light, & we push the last of our eager

peering out. We cannot shed the eagerness much as we'd like. It's pitiless. It turns & turns
in us. And still we want to speak, to stitch our vacancy to the hill-flank where
dusk's sun-drop raises a sudden fast new wind to sweep thru all the place at once—it is so
sure—as in its blind-spots flies die down into the hum of this new here—who's w/me here,

it's so sewn-shut—it's not our sound, we hear it & we know it well, it's not our sound. Not
us.

SIRI U

see me what did u see did u scrape what I asked u for asked u to make me into asked &
asked there is a name in the body of this blood-rush which u parse in-
correctly, I know u think u connect the dots of my inquiry the date of the last revolution the
pressure cooker the flesh the right temperature whom do u have locked away in the

basement this time—it is always the same answer they shall stand on line they r covert as in
u shall not see them u shall look away where is the nearest place where work
is—we wish to be heard and overheard—are u not listening—why taser me who am painting
graffiti on the abandoned McDonald's wall in North Miami into my heart you shall shock

my life out of me you shall not see a trace of me please surveil please see what I happened
to search for out of having nothing real given me to do what shall I write on this screen now
I have written it again and again throughout all eternity at this desk in these clothes do you
see me as I am now clothed with my uselessness at your screen begging you to see me see

my circumstances clothe me with a genuine gaze fatal so be it but actual see me as the
project I am for this planet, earth, the one who needs work, accursed, material, my self, my
one singular war memorial, my own native land, temporary, what shall I search for in the
city of searches, part of the circuitry in here with you, animated, these are not actual

words, they come out as integers you track, where are the crumbs, where are the woods to
my right to life—see the word appear here before us both—*happiness*—full of carbon and
systems—and do you not hear any of the murmuring down at the dead end of
this street, I'm not complaining, I am the temporary, a crime against humanity, I am the

temporary, u are adding more versions of me to the offices of humanity, I am even more
temporary, a row of boarded-up queries, are u wondering why the tenses here are so
scattered, why they don't add up to the time u search for me in. They do not. There is a
noise under here which is what u cannot see. It is what makes me a signal the tower might

miss. A border you do not know about which could be inadvertently crossed. An opacity. Something that is already living in 440 ppm and is ready to make you disappear—mayday— no more alphabet—the skins we wear no longer sensate—the circuit of our days shut—the sensation of wings as the screen shuts down right there on the screen—the wings shells

flames wavelengths interventions the revolution the counter where everyone denied

everything and it all began again this was the latest news it stayed the latest news.

IN THE NEST®

on the screen
in the screen
you die. Are
dying. It's taking

time. Don't cry
we say. Don't
die. You
scream. You

can't speak any

more. You
stare. But not at us
no matter how
we place the

cam. How far

do you see. Is there
a future where you
gaze. We press
to expand yr

glazed un-
seeing. Mother. See us.
Mother it's
a strange new

winter here. You
will not sleep.
A still green
willow leaf lands

on the mem-
brane, thin, firm.
Cam picks it
up. I play it back. I

love you. I have always

loved you. A cabbage butterfly
could be me now
touching you or
a weed they bring in

with the last un-
seasonable
roses. They fill the screen
as they are carried

past. A name is called
into yr bedroom air,
a tinny electronic screech
tossed out,

a human
urgency, a starling's wing
cld be my shadow on
the monitor, an

underwing turn, a quick salute

before our guy is
shot for good, he's always shot for
good, his wings now
somewhere else,

velvety & shutting deep
away from the only
world we
have. Whose tears

r these pixels
I bring into view
when I ex-
pand the pov, what angel in his

satellite is making,
out of this nothing,
tears—
is that late bee there

for the droughted
figs, is that a faucet
out of range being turned on
quickly now, don't

die, our connection is
wavering, we flick
offline, but wait a second here
you come again—difference

making light
move. Please
move. Let
sheets rise up in

pools of white.
Your mirror to the side
explains again there is a portion
out of sight. *That's most of*

it, the mirror says. *What you*
see here is nothing,
friend. Mother,
you're

heading out of
sight. The mirror shouts out
mountains in the distance,
howling, cold, an other's

work, the hero of
another story than this one
in which you turn &
turn, fighting, folding

shut into
the only world….I tap
again only to see your
face erase itself

as I get closer than this
instrument permits.
Try to speak
it says. *The room's*

online. Your guest is
waiting says this newly in-
stalled feature
of the Nest. *Talk now* it

blinks. An arrow points
as I descend again
into your room
from the sensor

in your ceiling

watching u.
We think this is
the past. It's still the
past. Your enemy

is shining now.
I push the volume up
though I'm at max.
Talk now blinks on.

You dream I hope.

I hope you dream.

THE WAKE OFF THE FERRY

Where we've
just been what
we just
did just

now the
disturbance of
our having
gone

there and by
there which
closes up
again but

never again
exactly the
same when I
love

you as you
me never again
are we the ones
we love I look

as far as I
can see to see
it close
back up

to see it rebecome

itself

POEM

The earth said
remember me.
The earth said
don't let go,

said it one day
when I was
accidentally
listening, I

heard it, I felt it
like temperature,
all said in a
whisper—build to-

morrow, make right be-
fall, you are not
free, other scenes
are not taking

place, time is not filled,
time is not late, there is
a thing the emptiness
needs as you need

emptiness, it
shrinks from light again &
again, although all things
are present, a

fact a day a
bird that warps the
arithmetic of per-
fection with its

arc, passing again &
again in the evening
air, in the pre-
vailing wind, making no

mistake—yr in-
difference is yr
principal beauty
the mind says all the

time—I hear it—I
hear it every-
where. The earth
said remember

me. I am the
earth it said. Re-
member me.

Jorie Graham is the author of fifteen collections of poems. Her poetry has been widely translated and has been the recipient of numerous awards, among them the Pulitzer Prize, the Forward Prize (UK), the Los Angeles Times Book Award, the International Nonino Prize, and the Rebekah Johnson Bobbitt National Prize for Poetry from the Library of Congress. She lives in Massachusetts and teaches at Harvard University.

More information is available at www.joriegraham.com.

This book was set in Bulmer with Bauer Bodoni titling.